Does God Wear Denim?

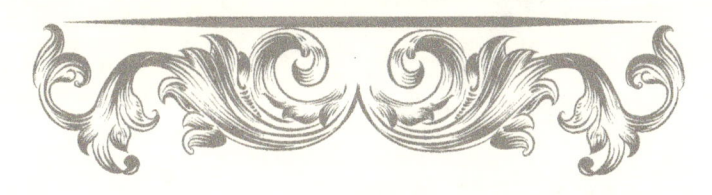

NETTA ABRAMS

ISBN 979-8-88751-261-7 (paperback)
ISBN 979-8-88751-262-4 (digital)

Copyright © 2023 by Netta Abrams

All rights reserved. No part of this publication may be reproduced, distributed, or transmitted in any form or by any means, including photocopying, recording, or other electronic or mechanical methods without the prior written permission of the publisher. For permission requests, solicit the publisher via the address below.

Christian Faith Publishing
832 Park Avenue
Meadville, PA 16335
www.christianfaithpublishing.com

Printed in the United States of America

Acknowledgments

First, I give thanks to the one who has held me in his hand before I had even existed, Father God (Yahweh) and Yashua Hamashiach (aka Jesus), who never forsake me.

My mother, I don't believe I would have made it, had you not started believing in me again while I was lost in the darkness during the aftermath. I love you so much.

My husband, Jesse, for the encouragement during my low points. Thank you for holding down the fort when I just didn't have the bandwidth to get this book completed.

My firstborn baby, Justin, your short life mattered. I love you.

My two additional gifts from God, Tia and Brandon, whom I was told would not make it, or would even be possible after this chapter in my life. I love you both now and forever.

A special thank-you goes out to Pastor Joseph, who asked me, "Have you ever heard of a sequel?" I know God spoke through you to get this story out after twenty-plus years of procrastination, I will *always* remember that phrase as I continue to write in the future.

CHAPTER 1

There may be a moment in a person's life when an unspeakable tragedy eventually comes to visit in a person's lifetime. If you are fortunate enough, there will be only one. For others, tragedy may come knocking on more than one occasion.

It's a time when living in turmoil, you are just trying to survive and swear that you will *never* look back at it again. In fact, you may walk around as if it didn't even happen (after the fact).

But it did happen. You are left picking up the pieces of a shattered outcome in hopes that you heal fast enough for the next blow that may come. Always being on your guard…what just happened? Why did this happen? This isn't the way it's supposed to happen, becoming isolated from just about every human being around you.

How will you escape? Is death a better option? Feels like the ground is swallowing you up. I know how that feels; I was there at one time. In fact, I was there more than one time.

Lightning doesn't strike a tree more than once, they say. Well, that isn't the way my life has gone. In fact, the lightning had struck too many times to count. Most of the strikes hit as a child and well into my twenties.

Tonight, I am going to share with you one of the biggest lightning strikes in my life. I am so very thankful to God that I was able to survive, heal, and be forgiven for it.

God has been asking me to write about this journey for the last twenty-seven years. I've given God every excuse as to why I couldn't do it. "I've never written a book," "I don't have the time," "I don't know what I am doing, or where to start." Now there are even more chapters to write about (as the lightning kept striking in my life).

He patiently waited, allowing me to escape the train wreck at hand. But he would also send me gentle signals that it was time—time to get up and write this book. There is a hurting, lost, overwhelmed person who needs to hear the message. Is this person you? Someone comes to mind that you may know?

Understand that God can work through *every* scenario if you surrender completely to him. There literally is *nothing* he cannot straighten out in a person's life if you would only let him. (I know… easier said than done.)

The time for excuses has now come to an end for me. He is not allowing me to "take another respite" from the worst event in my life to happen. This needs to get to someone very soon, and with God, it's all about the timing. He has now turned it up a notch by placing people in my path, songs on the radio, sermons in church or online that will bring up a topic that could easily fall in line with the events in my own life. As I am falling asleep, there is a stirring in my soul that is not quite describable that we are coming to a close soon when it comes to the dispensation of grace (the end of days).

If you are a nonbeliever that came across this book, the testimony I am about to dive into may help you or someone you know as well. You see, you can test him. Go ahead and test God. Watch what he is able to do. You will be simply amazed by the outcome. The odds of it coming out as you may expect won't always happen. But in the end, you will land on your feet, and he will have carried you the entire way.

For the believer who came across this book, my prayer is that it will be a confirmation of a sort that he is still near and he hears you.

We are going to take a walk together, and I will show you what it looks like to actually know Jesus rather than being religious. I hope by the end of this book, if anything, you will be able to see the difference between really knowing him and being religious. There is a *huge* difference.

Walking with a worldly title, such as a Christian, would look like to some people (that do not know him) as if we are judgmental, hypocritical, and in our Bible every day, putting on our armor of God to defeat the ugly sinners in the world by rebuking them to hell for what they have done in the name of Jesus, quoting scripture nonetheless. To the unbeliever, I am sure this is what it may look like.

What I am about to show you is far from being religious. It is about the vulnerable parts of walking with Jesus when you are in a place of darkness from which it appears as there is literally no escape. It's about him going in to rescue you when the darkness tells you lies like there is nowhere to turn. Forget about it, he will never come to get you now, deliver you the way you are, give up. he won't hear you—some of you in your walk on this planet may even question if he is even real at your point.

I've heard it all. The Bible is a bunch of fairy tales, Jesus was just some prophet. In some cases, I've heard "He isn't real." It's a made-up person to make a person feel better about what they are going through.

I am here to tell you he is *very* real, *always* present, and *will* rescue you from harm's way. But you will need to surrender it *all* to him and *believe* he will do it. Even if you can't see a way your circumstance would ever be able to change, do *not fear*. He is your safe haven.

To know him is not knowing nor even understanding the bible...at least, initially. The understanding of all that will come in time once your relationship is established. *But* you need to turn to him as is, as dirty as you think you are. As...you...are. He will come into your life and clean up the mess you are in. He will fill you up with the love you are missing and that you truly have never known to exist here on earth.

Walking with Jesus is not looking outward to what others are doing wrong and rebuking them with scripture. Walking with Jesus is very intimate; it is talking to him as you would anyone else (he hears you). It's asking him questions and waiting on him to answer you (time is involved in certain circumstances). Instead of praying for things to prosper, it's more like *what will you have me do today, Lord? Who can I reach today to glorify you?*

He does bless you as you walk with him. He loves you more than a parent would their own child (if you can believe that). Also... as a parent does a child, he will also discipline you if you fall off the right path he personally designed for you. This is out of love. If he didn't love you, he would be complacent and just let you go and run wild. If you decide to continue to rebel, he will allow it, and you will suffer the consequence of that decision to learn from it, and he will be waiting for you to return to him. Trying your best to not commit that same offense again...for some (like me), it will be impossible to break away from it without his help.

I believe if God or Jesus came back onto this planet in today's times...physically, he would be wearing denim. He is very much approachable, attainable, and is eager to walk alongside you no matter what the scenario.

Let's take a look at one of my own scenarios, shall we?

I won't get into the logistics of my upbringing (as that may be another book for another time). But I will say this. I was raised by a father that you would have thought was an alcoholic, but sadly wasn't. His abuse could not be blamed on alcohol. He came back from Vietnam and brought some demons along with him. He hypersexualized women, men's porn type magazines laying around the house for anyone to see. He had many triggers; you would never know when he was going to snap (very unpredictable). Sometimes months would go by, and other times, it would only take a matter of days. As a child, you never knew what it was that would set him off into gaslighting—sometimes a physical altercation of a sort, or verbal abuse. Being the only girl out of four kids didn't save me from my own biological father. If anything, looking back I think I may have gotten it the worst. However, I was also the eldest of the four of us and learned quickly that in order to survive his mind games, sexual and inappropriate behaviors with me (and yes, even physical abuse), I had to speak up right away and call it out (which didn't always end well for me either). It was for this reason I moved out shortly after I turned sixteen.

We had just moved to Las Vegas in the mid-'80s, and I can remember initially hating it there. There was a lot of moving around while growing up for me. My father could never hold down a job. Oh, how he struggled with his mental illness. All of us struggled with it—some of us more than others. Most of the stability for us kids was from my mother who always held down a job and ultimately was the breadwinner for the family.

As secure as that may seem, it also gave my father *lots* of opportunity to act out and abuse. There was a tremendous amount of gaslighting during this time as I would call him out for doing things to me. When Mom would come home, he would convince her that what I was saying was fabricated or even sometimes just made up. He would dismiss me often, and Mom would be so exhausted from her day's events, and trying to raise the four of us kids was more than what she could mentally handle. She would then have to deal with defending me or counseling my father and me.

I got tired of being a part of the circus. I would often lean on a boy I met in high school a lot, who also witnessed some of the abuse I endured. At the time, he had a place of his own (with roommates), but I liked having a place to run to if it got really bad. I could vent to him and also ease the burden from my mother. I spent almost all of my time over at his place.

Finally, the day had come where I was only able to bear the last blow from my father, and it was during one of his rants of "if you think you can have it better, then why don't you move out?"

That was a great idea, so I did. I moved into an efficiency apartment with Logan. At this time I was sixteen years old, held a full-time job, and went to high school at night time (SunSet High in Las Vegas). I started out pretty impressive for someone that age. After I moved out into my own place, I even made it on the honor roll.

My parents even bought us a Moped (scooter), so we could get around. Things were really working out nice, and I found an escape, but that would only prove to be temporary.

CHAPTER 2

A number of weeks had gone by (maybe a few months), and I started to come down with a flu bug perhaps. As the days had passed, it wasn't going away. I had developed stomach cramps. So much so that it brought me to what would be the first of many doctor visits.

This doctor, Dr. Black, scheduled my first ever D&C and laparoscopy. I arrived and went through the customary steps one would make to have this done. No education as to what to expect after this procedure. I was also put on birth control (which I didn't ask for, nor my mother either). I thought it was cool that I didn't even have to ask for it honestly. It was a relief that I didn't have to have awkward conversations with anyone to request it either.

That night I went home and bled bright red blood for several hours. I can remember staggering to the toilet to pee, and it kept coming out…bright red blood. Thinking this was normal, I went back to bed and slept it off. I didn't know it at the time, but this would be a defining moment that we call hemorrhaging.

I stayed at my parents' house overnight just in case something went haywire. By the next day, the bleeding had stopped.

Although I slept all night and was rather light-headed and groggy, again, I really thought that was normal. I went back to my apartment and started to pick up where I left off, went back to school, work, and loved my boyfriend.

I wasn't getting any better. In fact, I was slowly getting worse. I wasn't eating anymore, had off and on fevers, and was gaining weight (which made no sense to me whatsoever).

I can remember calling Dr. Black's office and leaving messages to call me back. I was confused. *Finally*, he called me back, and I gave him the scenario only to be met with condescending remarks such as "Maybe you have some kind of magical powers and are able to gain from not eating" type thing. I was shocked. I didn't know what to say at this point. I told my mom, who wasn't happy with that answer, and she knew enough to ask around at her work for any suggestions of a good ob-gyn.

She found one, Dr. Ester, and made an appointment for me to get in. However, this MD was so good, there would be a wait-list to get in to see her.

Needless to say, I didn't make that time frame. My health continued to deteriorate. There weren't any more home remedies that we could try (or over the counter meds). Mom called Dr. Ester's office and reported my symptoms that were worsening by the hour. I was on the floor with several blankets on me, shivering. Dr. Ester told my mom to bring me in that night, and she would meet us at her office (must have been about 8:00 p.m.). I remember it was dark out, and the MD had turned on the lights in her office. I was so sick yet impressed at the extent this doctor went to, to care for me. It was unreal.

Needless to say, I was a direct admit to the hospital from her office. I didn't even have time to go back home and change or pack a bag. Her office was located right next to the hospital. I got into my hospital gown and bed and was out for the night. Several tests were ordered for the very next morning.

The next morning arrived, and I was whisked away to radiology. I remember the ultrasound technician performing my test. I was looking at the monitor and saw this little white dot that kept getting bigger then little in rhythm. The tech's fun-loving joking she did with me at the beginning quickly changed to what I would say was a look of concern and a little of disbelief. I asked what that was flickering like that. She just blurted out, "You're pregnant!"

CHAPTER 3

I couldn't even believe my ears. My immediate reply was, "How is that possible!" I haven't had sex since the D&C! Not possible! She continued to roll over the area of my abdomen and then had to "make a call" as I was still and lay on the table. I was giddy with excitement (not the typical response of a teen in those days). I thought immediately that this had to be an absolute miracle! The baby lived through a D&C and laparoscopy! Incredible news! I can't wait to tell the world! I am witnessing a miracle of God!

In that moment of time all I thought about was how incredibly blessed I was, forgetting about my deteriorating health. So…much… joy! I couldn't wait to tell Logan and then my family. After all, I was managing an apartment, school, and job. I just knew I could do this!

Again, I was forgetting about being so sick: not able to go to school for a time, calling in sick because I was getting dizzy spells, not always able to comprehend what was said to me, and maybe even having to forfeit my apartment because I was getting so sick, Logan and I could no longer take care of myself (I was that sick).

I gave Logan the good news; he was stunned yet excited. We just knew we could do this. After all, we had our shit together. Together, we announced that we were going to have the baby (and giving him up wasn't an option). My parents didn't receive the news as I anticipated. Initially, there was silence on the other end of the phone… no response. Then a halfhearted, "Oh wow" from my mom (I'm sure she was in shock). I tried to explain what a miracle this was and how God brought this life to me as a gift. Granted, I was very ill, but I just knew in my heart: it would all work out and be okay.

Logan's parents received the news even worse than my parents did. His mother never really liked me, and without hesitation, offered him a bus ticket back to Missouri to get away from me. She told him that I was going to ruin his life, take him down, and he would never amount to anything if he stayed with me.

On that note, I was released from the hospital in stable condition (after having several IVs of fluids and antibiotics, yet another risk to a baby) and came back to my parents' house for follow-up care. Still sick and starting back down the road to failing health, the fevers returned with more vengeance. I was spending several hours lying on the floor next to the toilet for some comfort, and this way, I didn't have to keep running to the bathroom.

I can remember vomiting my guts out and shivering from fever at the same time, and my father was standing in the doorway, laughing at me and telling me this is what I get for making the choices I did.

Another follow up visit to the MD after the release from the hospital would bring me to a crossroad that I never thought I would have to face. For me, it was never a second thought or doubt. My baby would be here within a number of months. The doctor told me that I needed to give the baby up (I was about three months pregnant at this time).

I told her that I would not be "giving him up." Even if that means I would die by bringing him into the world. Wasn't...going...to...happen. Period.

I went back to my parents' house, and by this point, I had been sick for several weeks now. We lost our apartment; we both moved in with my parents, all the while hearing how we shouldn't have this baby. I fought for the baby as I continued to deteriorate. God, I know you are with me and you want me to keep it. The baby would have not made it this far if it wasn't meant to be. You and I are close. I know what I am witnessing is nothing more than a miracle. Give me the strength to stay the course.

The fevers continued, and I was getting worse. I can remember one morning I was lying down in the living room, and my father was sitting in the recliner reading a newspaper, slowly turning the pages. I remember asking him a question. He didn't respond, or look at me… nothing. I thought that maybe he didn't hear me the first or second time, so I got up off the couch and hobbled over to him. I looked at him and asked the same question. It was if I wasn't even there…like I did not exist. He just kept calmly turning the pages of the paper and continued to read. Mom and Logan were at work, and my brothers were in school. It really felt like I didn't even exist anymore.

On another occasion I received a letter from my aunt in Wyoming telling me I should be happy that the baby has to go because I was like a baby having a baby type scenario.

This kind of "support" was killing me slowly, along with the illness. Mom and I were close, but she didn't have many words for me during that time either.

Finally, the day arrived that I was so sick, I wound up back in Dr. Ester's office again. A verbal fight ensued. It was once again when everyone was gone, and she had told me point blank that I had to sign the papers and they needed to take the baby. I responded as I always had from the time I found out that the baby was on the way. This was a witnessed miracle, and I will die for this baby if need be.

She walked over and calmly shut the door. She said "Listen, this will not ever go beyond these four walls. God meant for you to have a healthy baby! It was a man who went in there and fucked it all up! Your uterus sounded to ten centimeters…anything over eight indicates pregnancy, and he should have stopped then and let things be. But he didn't. He kept going.

"Here are the scenarios that you are facing: you could die, and the baby could live. You and the baby may not make it (my preferred method—all or nothing). You both could live, and he could be so disfigured and have a normal brain and hate you for bringing him into the world. He could have severe mental disability and disfigurement, and you could die…" The list was endless.

It was as if God was speaking to me through the doctor. I did not want to do it, but then caved and went ahead and signed the paperwork. I then asked her when she was going to do it.

Her response? "Oh, I'm not going to do it. I don't have anything to do with that. I know someone who does and will send you over to him." By now, I was within weeks of approaching five months. Still very sick, pale, and weak…

It was at this point I realized that aside from Logan, I had no one…but God.

CHAPTER 4

I had grown to trust Dr. Ester in a very short period of time. At this point, I wasn't looking forward to meeting with this next doctor. Another complete stranger. My mother also had to jump several hoops to get this done as well. Letters had to be written from Doctor Ester in order to have this done. I was already far along in my pregnancy. The state wouldn't allow it at the time unless my life was in jeopardy.

Mom had set up the appointment for me. It wouldn't be long now before the baby was going to be leaving. Every night I spoke to him and rubbed my belly. I apologized for what I was about to do. I believe I also asked God for forgiveness. I knew his days were numbered, and part of me was already hoping to go along with him (ending my own life with his).

I showed up for my appointment. My mom was alongside me. I signed the papers and an initial review of my medical records that led me all the way up to his office. After that meeting, I was taken to a room with a nurse who gave me the usual instruction of changing into a hospital gown.

Not being experienced by this kind of thing and at such a low point in my life, I had asked if this was it. Are we doing this right now? This is going too fast. She told me that this wasn't "it," that I just needed to have a seaweed pellet put up into my cervix to help me dilate when the time comes (this was to remain in place for three days).

I got up onto the table and lay there, waiting for them to insert it. Once they did it, it literally took my breath away in a stabbing pain. It lasted for several minutes before it subsided. I was sent home with my mom and went back to bed.

I spoke a lot to the baby—our last night together. I lay there in the still of the night, just the two of us, and I rubbed my belly, apologized, and made a promise that everyone will know about him. That he once lived, and that we loved each other. I also promised that if he had any siblings, they would grow up knowing he was first.

After the three-day period of time, the terrible day had arrived. It was time for the baby to go back to heaven. This was going to be an outpatient procedure. The instructions were like all the prior ones: here is your gown, here is the remote should you need anything. The IV was started. For the nurse, it was like business as usual, just like over at the clinic.

Mom and Logan were with me when I went in to have it done. It was a dimly lit room. I think something like *The Price Is Right* was playing in the background. The nurse educated me on what I can expect as things move along. They were inducing labor via IV, I had the seaweed pellet in, and once that slides out, they will know that things are really moving along at a pretty good clip.

Just the way the nurse was running through the protocol was kind of cold and business as usual. I told her my story of how life had brought me to this point, and that this was not something I even wanted to do in the first place. She seemed to have warmed up to me then.

The IV was started. Logan, Mom and myself were just talking for about an hour when things really started picking up. I was getting my first contractions. I felt like I had to go to the restroom. I got up with help from Logan and plopped down on the toilet.

I was going to the bathroom, when out of nowhere there was an intense feeling of pushing, and I did what my body was telling me to do. I heard a splash into the toilet. I lost my mind at this point. I didn't even want to look. I thought it was the baby. I felt a little body slide on out with that push (or so I imagined). Screaming for my mom to get the nurse, I didn't want to look. The nurse came in and looked down into the toilet and reassured me it wasn't the baby. It was the seaweed pellet. I gently walked with the nurse on one side and Logan on the other back to my gurney bed.

Things were going fast now. I wanted to push again. As soon as I got to the bed the (the MD had stopped in right before this), I was told by the nurse that I couldn't push until the MD had gotten to my room. He had figured that this was my first baby and would take longer to get to this point. He went to lunch, and I had to cross my legs until he arrived. I was completely hysterical by this point. I could literally feel him slide down the birth canal and stop right at the opening. All it would take me was one big push, and I just knew he would be out.

Finally, the doctor had arrived back and got his OR gear on. They had wheeled me back to the OR suite and knocked me out on the way in. I woke up in recovery and had no idea what was going on. And just like that, the baby was no more.

I asked the nurse what sex the baby was. Initially, she refused to tell me what it was, but after enough begging and pleading and I needed to give "it" a name, she had told me it was a boy. Two pounds two ounces and appeared completely normal. I couldn't bear him being thrown into the trash (like you see in those grotesque pictures). She told me that they had donated him to the medical college. I am assuming he is in a jar of formaldehyde in a college somewhere (which is better than the trash).

After that, I was on my way home. Logan was also a bit traumatized as well. He told me that he had peeked in the room I was in for the abortion and saw blood all over everything.

Now I was supposed to act normal because after all, to everyone else this was a blessing for me, and I could just move on now with no problem. They couldn't be further from the truth. My nightmare was only gaining ground on me. As I slipped away from everyone mentally in my mind, I found a very dark corner there where I would take up residence for a season. I was now as far down as anyone could be.

CHAPTER 5

It was at this point that I completely shut down. The baby's name was Justin Michael. I would have visions of Justin covered in blood in my bedroom closet, lying in a pool of blood, asking why I did it. I totally felt defeated as I had let God down in the battle of keeping him. I carried a lot of guilt for many, many years, but it was the absolute worst within the year of his death.

I didn't really have any closure for my baby boy. I asked the Holy Spirit to help me have a funeral for him. I bought a pacifier and tied a blue shoestring to it to resemble him. I said several prayers that day and tried really hard to forgive myself for what had just happened.

As for everyone else, they were carrying on as if it was just another day. I would sit for hours in the dark without anyone even aware I was gone. I can remember sitting in my bedroom closet with the door closed, just crying. I couldn't even feel God's presence at the time.

I did make an attempt at going back to school after this, but didn't really feel like I fit in anymore. I just sat quietly in the classroom. It's all a blur.

I got sick again. The infection I had before when I was pregnant came back with a vengeance. Back in the hospital I went. I initially had my own room until they brought another woman in to share a room with me who, in her fifth month, was having preterm labor. Not really sure who was making assignments that day, but that wasn't a very good idea. The woman was in travail with her labor, and the night ultimately ended with her delivering her baby right in that bed next to me. It was a girl. The nurses did not come in there that often to be with her. I had a very hard time listening to the pain coming from her right next to me.

But I do remember talking her through it. She lost her baby that day. They brought the stillborn back to her after cleaning it. I could hear their goodbyes to the baby, and they got to plan a funeral for her.

As much as I was able to help her, there I was slipping further and further away mentally. I can remember during yet another hospitalization where I had some of my classmates (quite a group of them) visit me and brought me a cactus with squiggly eyes. That sticks out to me because it was around that time when I realized that I wasn't going to make it in school anymore either. I tried to go back, but would be too sick to continue (at this point mentally and physically).

I quit school in tenth grade, stopped eating, and lay in an upstairs bedroom, praying for death in the dark. I could only stare at the ceiling and ask God to bring me home. If I was honest, I was begging for that.

I wanted to die. I didn't deserve to live without my baby. To make matters even worse, I was told I probably couldn't carry another child to full term due to the scarring that happened to me. The infection ravaged my body, mind, and spirit.

Here I was, completely isolated, a dropout, overwhelmed, and still, the battle raged on. It just…wouldn't…end. I was so sick of being sick, missed my son so badly. Almost every time I tried to get back into my life and start back up again, I would see a baby that would be around Justin's age, and it would throw me right back into isolation.

CHAPTER 6

Finally, I came up with a plan. God, you refuse to bring me home with my baby. I plan on meeting you face-to-face, so we could have a discussion. I now had a plan in place. I wanted to make it painful for punishment. I wouldn't be able to get out of it once I started it, and no one would find me until it was too late, and I would have already been dead. I was to light myself on fire in a cornfield, and I will leave a letter where they would find me. It was sealed. The decision was made. I was going to die soon.

I really felt unworthy, beaten up, thrashed around. The continued happiness around me wouldn't stop. Even if it was because Justin was now gone, I felt like the joy that everyone had was because I gave him up, and now they didn't have to worry about that. It would be easy for them now.

My mother must have somehow picked up on this because she had me in counseling. She went with me. I believe the counselor didn't really believe that I would do it. He looked over at my mom and asked her if she thought I would. There was a long pause, and she had said yes. "Yes, I think she might." That was surprising to me because I was so low at this point. No one believed in me anymore, even with death. I couldn't wait to leave the world and be with Jesus and Justin. I had a plan but didn't really have a date set yet.

CHAPTER 7

Shortly after the planned period of time, as I was praying for courage to go through with it, I once again got sick. I had so much abdominal pain. This time I was in the ER, and they were not planning on admitting me (for once). They gave me a shot to ease the pain and said I could go back home.

My parents and Logan were there with me. Off I went, hopping into the backseat of my parents' hatchback with Logan. Mom was up front to the right, and my dad was driving. Once I got settled in the car, I noticed my heart was racing. Kind of like if you would run quite a distance nonstop. I had raised my hand over my mouth to check and see if I would have been hyperventilating. Nope, that wasn't the case either. Now at this point I had a feeling like I might be dying. As I was losing consciousness, I leaned forward and told my mom that I was going to hang on as long as I can. I was out, but the weird part about this is that I could still hear everything that was going on. I heard my mom yell at my dad to turn the car around. Then I heard the car door open and people calling my name, slapping my face to get me to "wake up," and then heard, "I can't find a pulse." They lifted me out of the back seat of the car, threw me in a wheelchair, and ran into the ER. I heard a lot of movement and talking back and forth between the nurses. Like "Is she always this pale?" The nurse that gave me the shot stated yes, I looked pale, but maybe not as pale.

Then God spoke to me lovingly and yet stern. There was a window which he would allow me to come home. All I had to do was relax and go with it. Do not resist it. *But* if I am out (out of my body), I will not be allowed to return. Once I am out, I am out, and that will be it. God was offering me my long-awaited wish! I couldn't believe it! Right after this invitation was given to me as a painless death and to move back home, I also remember hearing my mother and Logan in the background as well. Could I leave them? I was surprised by my own choice. It turned out that I really did want to live! I felt what could be described as a roundness like the tip of a vacuum hose pulling at me gently from right below my ribcage. Just as if a vacuum cleaner suction was trying to pull me out of my body. Inside I resisted it. I held on for dear life in my body. God had revealed to me that I really didn't want to die after all. He gave me an open window, and I didn't take it. I passed up that wonderful opportunity to go home and be with him.

The thought of leaving my mother and boyfriend at that time meant more to me when given the choice. When I came to, my face was itchy, I had blankets on me, and the crash cart was out right next to me. They were pulling the cover off of it as I gazed over. They were asking me questions like who was the president and what year it was, etc. My face was so itchy. I passed out and was admitted again. I felt a gentle hand brushing the hair out of my eyes. I said, "Mom? Mom?" There was no response. When I opened my eyes, the room was pitch-black, with the exception that I could see the light coming from underneath the door. After all that I had been through, I do believe it was an angel sent to comfort me.

It has been a very long journey finding my way back to Jesus. This is just a snapshot of one of many chapters in my life. After this period of time, I continued to be in and out of hospitals and clinics for a number of years, battling infections. Finally, I overcame that part of my life. It was a pivotal moment, and I have never been the same since that period of time.

CHAPTER 8

But God—
 Jesus has never left me. He was there by my side through it all. That's having a relationship, not religious. It was him and I on many nights…no one else. At that period of time in my life I barely read scripture, if at all. It was just me crying out to him almost every night and praying to him. He would pull me out of several poor decisions I had made after losing Justin as well (again, another book for another time).

The road is long with many hills and valleys. Having children didn't look like it was in the cards for me after that happened.

But God, granted I was considered high risk and hemorrhaged during both my pregnancies—I have two grown healthy children now.

GED: I never did get to graduate from high school. Made it to tenth grade, took my GED when I was seventeen years old. Started working toward a nursing degree at twenty-three years old in 1989 without getting into the additional roadblocks on that journey. *Finally* graduated with an associate's degree in nursing in December 2003. Two more degrees in nursing followed, one in 2010, a bachelor's in nursing, and then a master's in nursing 2013.

God *will* restore what had been taken from you and add to it. He *will*. But you need to surrender to him. It will take faith for sure. It may take time (sometimes months or years).

I lost so much in my life, but as the years pass by, they have also been restored. There have been seasons when it seemed like Jesus left me, but I was wrong. It was the other way around. I would always find my way back to him, and he would restore me and my repentant broken heart. If I were a religious person, I would feel like I would burn in hell for this and never come back from the sin in my life. But I am not religious. I have a relationship with Jesus and understand that he died for my sin, so that I may live my life walking with him, serving him, and fellowshipping with him.

My father has since passed away, and even he was restored. A few months before his death, he also accepted Jesus's invitation of deliverance and was forgiven. He was a completely changed man: the father I always wanted. We reconciled. He passed weeks later.

If God was to appear today, he would be wearing denim, not a high-end suit. Totally approachable. He *will* meet you where you are *today*. You are totally missing out on an incredible relationship. Do not pass it up.

Thank you for taking the time to accept my invitation to walk with Jesus and I during that window of time.

Netta's lessons

Why do people get sick and sometimes die? There are people that you need to meet and come into contact with, and you wouldn't ever get to meet them unless the sickness or death didn't happen. God uses *everything* for a purpose. I believe that our date and time of death is prewritten before we are even born. We each have a job that we have to do here for the glory of our Father. Once our job is completed, we get to go home. Some of our jobs are shorter than others. You just need to hold onto the thought that a person who died would have still died on that particular day no matter how. It was already ordained before we were born.

Babies die with a purpose. My son had a short job to do while here. He made a big impact on me, and when I give my testimony, it has helped others while they are on their life journey as well. I will get to see him again. He is in the best place anyone could imagine.

Our children are not ours to keep. We are assigned the caretakers of children, and they are gifts of time to us. All people are God's creation and will return to him in the end. Some for reward and some for judgment. But we all return back to him.

Are you saved? If you *know* Jesus, you are one of the lucky few. Most proclaiming Christians do not know him, but know his words very well and are big fans of his. You could compare that to someone who knows all the words to a favorite singer's song and knows everything about that singer, but do they know that singer personally? Does the singer know them? Not really. The same scenario happens to Jesus over and over again. People know about him, but have they spoken to him every day? Thanked him daily? Brought their troubles to him and said they are sorry if they had hurt him?

How do you get saved? Understand that we all fall short from perfect. Jesus doesn't expect you to be perfect. He died for the sin we have done. He knows that our flesh is weak. It's okay. Turn to him as you are. He loves you so much. He will strengthen you, refine you, forgive you. He wants you to keep trying to follow him every day. If you stumble, it's okay. He knows you are doing your best. It's called picking up our cross (past pain, sin, temptations) and surrendering them over to him. To surrender is to try your best every day to live by following his commandments. The commandments were given to help us stay on the narrow path by keeping us out of trouble.

Turn to him now. How do you turn to him and get saved? Run to him today and tell him that you understand that you are a sinner. That you have sinned against him whether you were aware or not, and you are sorry that you did that (purposeful or not). You also understand that he had taken up your sin and paid the price for it by dying on the cross. Ask him for forgiveness and to deliver you from evil of any kind. Ask him to walk with you as you go forward, with him guarding your steps along the way.

I am praying for the readers of this book. Here is my prayer for you:

> Dear heavenly Father, Adoni, please bless this reader right now. I pray for wisdom in these last

days, for relationships if they don't know you. For a rekindling of a relationship if they somehow got lost, and a strengthening bond for those who do know you. Please cover them under your wing when they need refuge and protection for them and their families. Father, I don't know their hearts, but you do. You know and understand what their needs are better than they do. Father, I thank you for the reader of this book and also thank you in advance that you have this person in your hand and are waiting for them patiently with a love that is incomprehensible to turn to you. Thank you and praise you in Jesus's mighty name. Amen.

Peace be with you reader. Shalom.

About the Author

Netta Abrams is a budding new author. After much encouragement from friends and family, along with strong guidance from Father God, she is sharing part of her testimony in this book, hoping to help others who may have lost their way or have never had a relationship with Jesus to be able to find him. She is currently working as a registered nurse in Texas. Netta has a husband of twenty-two years. She is a mom and a Mi-Mi of three.

CPSIA information can be obtained
at www.ICGtesting.com
Printed in the USA
JSHW080716270423
40911JS00002B/90

9 798887 512617